JANUARY

SHORT POEMS OF NEW ZEALAND

EDITED BY
JENNY BORNHOLDT

VICTORIA UNIVERSITY PRESS

TE WHARE WĀNANGA O TE ŪPOKO O TE IKA A MĀUI
VICTORIA
UNIVERSITY OF WELLINGTON

VICTORIA UNIVERSITY PRESS
Victoria University of Wellington
PO Box 600 Wellington
vup.victoria.ac.nz

First published 2018

A catalogue record is available from the National Library of New Zealand

ISBN 9781776562022

Printed in China by 1010 Printing International

Introduction

I've begun to think of short poems as being the literary equivalent of the small house movement. Small houses contain the same essential spaces as large houses do. Both have places in which to eat, sleep, bathe and sit; the difference being that small houses are, well, smaller. Like the question of bathrooms—does one need six stanzas or will one do? What short poems might lack in floor space they make up for in nifty storage. You might have to go outside to swing the cat, but you can still have the thought indoors.

I began collecting poems for this book in 2010, but life stuck its nose in and the brown manila folder I'd jammed an assortment of poems into didn't surface again until mid-2017. When I looked at the poems I'd chosen—among them work by Mary Ursula Bethell, Sam Hunt, Michelle Amas and Geoff Cochrane—all remained lively and interesting to me, so I began gathering others, aware that at some stage I would have to decide just how short was short.

I was briefly tempted to limit myself to poems of six lines and under. This proved to be too restrictive, so I tried ten. After more reading, ten lines seemed too long to be properly short, so I settled on nine. Many poets write ten-line poems—five two-line stanzas are commonplace. Ten lines feel roomy; there's space to write concisely about something and feel you've covered the territory. It's trickier to wrangle a feeling, a narrative, an event, a thought, into nine lines, though this anthology shows that many writers have done so in a great variety of voices.

These poems relate stories, describe memorable scenes, set off emotional grenades, sense death, declare love, make jokes. They talk about cities and forests, tower blocks, airports and beaches, cars and picnics.

When it came to ordering the anthology I enjoyed the way poems acted as magnets to others. There are gatherings of writing about cars, sport, war, love, loss, nature, history, people wronged—all of life. The poems are grouped loosely into five sections and I hope that each one reads as a book within a book.

Janet Frame's poem 'The Chickadee' opens the selection. It's a poem about imagination as a living thing that needs attention and care. All poets, all writers, tend to thought and language. As readers of this anthology, you do the same valuable work.

Jenny Bornholdt

The Chickadee

The chickadee drops like a scroll out of the sky,
Alights on my hand. I feed him sunflower seeds.
The inky brushmarks on his head are scarcely dry.

Janet Frame

from The Harbour Poems

The blue agapanthus, the yellow fennel, the white
butterfly, the blue harbour, the golden grass,
the white verandah post, the blue hills, the yellow
leaves, the white clouds, the blue
book, the yellow envelope, the white paper.
Here is the green verb, releasing everything.

Dinah Hawken

Haiku (1)

Stop
your snivelling
creek-bed:

come rain hail
and flood-water

laugh again

Hone Tuwhare

Balagan

is a Hebrew word
meaning ‘total chaos’.

Balagan balagan balagan
balaganbalaganbalaganbalagan

Stop. All is still.
Begin again.

Frances Samuel

Everest

conversation overheard on bus

It's the Palagi
getting around
wanting to touch everything
in this world.
Touching, touching everything
Look at that one with no legs—
walked right up that hill

Therese Lloyd

The avalanche

Who is enormous? The mountain. The sky.
Who holds who up? I want to fall into crevices,
I want to be buried, only to be found,
this is the miracle, to walk as if alive.
What?
Is this tomorrow?
Are these, paws?

Maria McMillan

Beach

Languages on a blue t-shirt
take us to the edge of English.
At night, the sea is close to our bedroom.
We worry that there is a dog next door.
In the sand, we find prints
of our own feet.

Mary Macpherson

The City from the Hills

There lies our city folded in the mist,
Like a great meadow in the early morn
Flinging her spears of grass up through white films,
Each with its thousand thousand-tinted globes.

Above us such air as poets dream,
The clean and vast wing-winnowed clime of Heaven.

Each of her streets is closed with shining Alps,
Like Heaven at the end of long plain lives.

Arnold Wall

Wellington at 5 O'Clock

Where they might stand and throw
Applecores down ships' funnels,
People walk dully home
Up steps, or go through tunnels.

Denis Glover

Foreshore, Evening

An over-done town picnic:
pets, furniture, makeshift beds,

                                        cooking fires.

                News or rumours
passing along the sand,

ladies asleep with their hats on.

Anna Livesey

Home Thoughts

I do not dream of Sussex downs
or quaint old England's
quaint old towns—
I think of what may yet be seen
in Johnsonville or Geraldine.

Denis Glover

Introductions

I have never lived in Palestine
but I did grow up in Gisborne
                And I have never had a hangi-in-a-pie
but I do know where to get one

Louise Wallace

Cookbook

At Sunday School
I rose to read:
Sure to Rise.

Murray Edmond

Cromwell

is a town of Greek summers
and rock-splitting winters.

I should know,
I was born not far from there.

So who's the guy on the poncy
horse outside Westminster?

Bernadette Hall

In the Younger Land

This stubborn beach, whereon are tossed
white roses from the sea's green bough,
has never sheathed a Norman prow
nor flinched beneath a Roman host;

yet in my bones I feel the stir
of ancient wrongs and vanished woes,
and through my troubled spirit goes
the shadow of an old despair.

A.R.D. Fairburn

Rain over Mitimiti Mountains

A grey stole of weather drawn from sky to sea,
White-furred with mist trailing on mountain ledges;
The clouded harbour breathes lightly as rain.
A horseman slowly passing lifts his hand
In silent greeting, but does not pause or turn.
Beneath the infinite whorls of Whiria Pa Hill
Pipi-gatherers stray about the wet shore.

Charles Brasch

I asked for riches
you gave me
scavenging rights on a far beach

Keri Hulme

Sitting in front of the Karetu Marae

Ngati Manu's flag hugs the staff.
Ping pong in the dining hall.

The sun spills light over the hills across
The creek. A horse flicks its tail.

The door to Grandad's house is shut.
Ten goats nuzzle on a higher hill.

A dog rolls in front belly up.
This day fills us: slow breeze in a cloth.

Robert Sullivan

Lord Cobham Avenue

a birthday next door
and a visiting
grandmother here

we spend the afternoon
lifting small girls
over the fence

Tony Beyer

Bring your camera ay?

Morning shadows reach across
the dirt and sawdust of Robert
Rex's backyard. Two men in
faded shorts, wet sandshoes
their faces show the weight of
pa'ala and yellowfin tuna
on a pole that sags between them.
A black dog shooed away, still gets
its arse in the corner of the shot.

Rob Hack

Savvy meters clack their blank eyes shut.

No one arrives and no one departs;
the walls are full of dice and knucklebones;
mice snack on quiet's little bongos.

When aqueous day eventuates
and light lies like water on the tiles,
yellow birds will sip
from morning's shallow stoup

Geoff Cochrane

Big City Rush Hour

Cloud pops out,
a body-builder posing.
Heat grills each car on the grid,
bronze light slashes off the windows.
A bus sways forward concertina-style.
A finance house stacks up its cool vertical lines,
calculator-thin.
This town stands as open as an airport lounge,
Everyone looks like a new arrival.

David Eggleton

When I came to your shore
I was a nobody
I had no name
I am what you call a stateless man
I was blind
but then I touched this soil
I saw a moon
I had an immense feeling

John Pule

Motel

The blue lights of the Airport Motor Lodge:
they cobalt me; they penetrate and stain;
they send me, yes, and bring me back again.

Geoff Cochrane

Roadkill

fleece fur feather
petrol fumes
hard rubber wheels
and leather

David Eggleton

Bumper stickers

Some of the world's least pleasant thoughts
find their way onto bumper stickers.

Worse—
most are not funny so

don't laugh
your daughter might be inside.

Kate Camp

Tony's Tyre Service

Tony's Tyre Service is customer-focused. When they change
        my tyres
they also freshen up my car's interior. I like these guys

and their amiable TV commercial is a song-and-dance hoot.
Tony—listen to me: I can sing along. I hope you read this,

Tony, and give me a break. I'm bald
and stale and need a cheerful tune.

Ian Wedde

Referee

he needs to let the game go
he needs to go back to Townsville
he needs to know we didn't drive seven hours
to listen to him play his whistle.

Hinemoana Baker

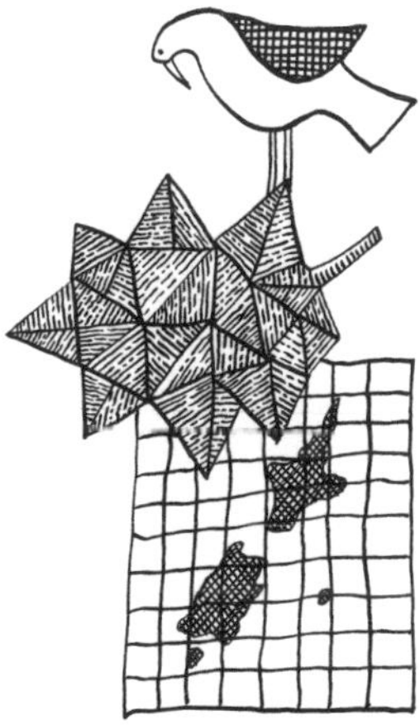

Dreams, Yellow Lions

When I was young
I used to dream of girls
and mountains.

Now it is water I dream of,
placid among trees, or lifting
casually on a shore

where yellow lions come
out in the early morning
and stare out to sea.

Alistair Te Ariki Campbell

On Turning Seventy

I think it came to me in sleep
that when at Anzac dawn parades
old soldiers weep
it’s not as they will say for fallen comrades

but for the young self full of sap and fire
as distant now and caught in coils of time
as one the bullets of some half-forgotten war
stopped in his prime.

C.K. Stead

East Belfast

Birds sit in trees older than me.
There's a church older than my country.
Tourists are taking pictures
of a mural, what's left of one:
release our something *men*,
we shall something *up*.

Lynley Edmeades

My World War I Poem

Inside each trench, the sound of prayer.
Inside each prayer, the sound of digging.

Bill Manhire

Suicide Abroad

You buy bullets
Which lie on your palm like money.
You owe them nothing.

To release a captive sparrow
Is prayer. You meet your agent at dawn
Amid fragile cages of song.

Geoff Cochrane

Anorexia

electric doors
don’t sense her

Frances Samuel

A Small Seascape in Oils

Instead of fruit, furniture or flesh
Squall, cloudburst and stain
Are the seascape accoutrements.

Squall is a window, cloudburst the action
In still life seen in wrung-neck fowls
Or limp rabbits hung up by their feet.

Stain and shadow are the flesh tints
Waves wear to delineate their form
The way nudes bend to pick up their shoes.

Elizabeth Smither

cherry pie

deeper and deeper
here are the fields of falling nerves
here are the lanes of sour smells
we are muddy and twisted and green
we are familiar and bright and peeling

Paula Green

Cape Gooseberries

for Lynn

I think of the Cape Gooseberry
In its little house of sighs,

A lantern of good intentions
Pulsing the veined husk,

A flare-up on the tongue
Extinguishing pleasure.

Chris Orsman

Waiting for my brother

I kill wasps
between copies of *Samoan Custom*
and *Flotsam and Jetsam from the Pacific Ocean*.

There is a line of the dead
above my head as I sleep.
My brother will have to
make his own arrangements.

Tusiata Avia

On Rapanui (Easter Island)

The great voyages of Polynesian history, of Cook
and La Pérouse and Thor Heyerdahl's Kon-Tiki
    as nothing compared

to the everyday transit, by Southern Pacific Gyre
of one bucket, a left-footed jandal and two plastic containers
marked 'Property of Sanfords, South Island, New Zealand'.

Gregory O'Brien

Remembering Mrs Hardy

All the dozen or so blue miles
  into the town were a joy,
those miles beneath the simplest sky
  easing my way

to the one man I loved, the one
  I would have eaten grass for.
And the miles back, the unending red miles
  of what I let myself in for.

Vincent O'Sullivan

High Country Weather

Alone we are born
   And die alone;
Yet see the red-gold cirrus
   Over snow-mountain shine.

Upon the upland road
   Ride easy, stranger:
Surrender to the sky
   Your heart of anger.

James K. Baxter

Friend:

This is the dearest of my wishes,
The last leaf shaken from the tree:
Sow the southerly with my ashes
To fall in tears on Kapiti.

Alistair Te Ariki Campbell

Poem

When we touch,
forests enter our bodies.

The dark wind shakes the branch.
The dark branch shakes the wind.

Bill Manhire

Under Erebus

A woman is standing under Erebus.
She has wrapped all her gifts around her,
including *caritas*.

A bulky mammal able to feed her young.

See the red flag with its purple shadow,
the flagged road curving towards tomorrow.

There is shelter here, off to the right,
a bunch of metal rods and a cloth.

You wonder if it's going to be enough.

Bernadette Hall

Temporary Beds

This is our year of changing circumstance
I will make four homes for you,
your bed will be a compass in this city.

To every bedroom you will bring
the same sock, the same piece of fluff, a corner
of paper and River Phoenix.

I will bring an umbrella ceiling
to hold over you at night
to keep the dark from falling.

Michele Amas

Ariel

Something that rises
beneath the curved
ribs, catching the
updraft of vision.
Unending kite
on the string
of love.

Bob Orr

What Licence Issued You Away?

Things have changed since you were with us.
We no longer call a spade a spade.

Now we say you are crazy and try to believe it.
Now we say 'she loved us then', and 'there can be no return'.

Connection, light as sunlight through clouds;
as light's flick across valleys, across gorse.

There is no way of saying we are sorry, save to hold you.
There is no way to hold or save you.

Anna Livesey

Sapwood and Milk

I should not have known you
were it not for bowers
indecorously fashioned to such
coarse bowing and trampling
subtle belling of leaves
squinch of grass. And in the

Lilt and mesh of eyes
golden slices of the peach-moon's
merriment

Hone Tuwhare

22 March '96

Sleep is the avenue of
Linden trees when the sun is
unrelenting.

Sleep is the parcel
addressed to someone else.

Rachel Bush

Wild Iron

Sea go dark, dark with wind,
Feet go heavy, heavy with sand,
Thoughts go wild, wild with the sound
Of iron on the old shed swinging, clanging:
Go dark, go heavy, go wild, go round,
Dark with the wind,
Heavy with the sand,
Wild with the iron that tears at the nail
And the foundering shriek of the gale.

Allen Curnow

Panther

panther water
iron black

when I turn my back
you reach for me

ah! the cold

I turn to you
I turn to you

Sarah Broom

Still

Still as, no just still
as if the world ends
at these white curtains
and a sign would say,
Here be dragons.
This quiet centre.
This still unfeeling heart,
exact, precise, terminal.

Rachel Bush

Watching the Hawkduns

Look, let your eye track them, eastward and back,
Rucking their curtains along winter's rack.

Vincent O'Sullivan

I was born with
wings in my hands

What did I do wrong
what did I say to
upset the gods

Why do they want
me back

John Pule

Carved Couple

When he flies with her in the far angle
of a roof there is no one but her.

Their eyes, four strokes of the same
chisel. And she is saying—

in the recessed flanking places
where you find them—

my stone mouth is halfway,
love, to yours.

Diana Bridge

'You're Just a Dreamer'

Where are my ancestors now
people with my crude name
and changing eye-colour?

They are lost, through too much
looking at the sea.
People everywhere now are cleverer.

How in Heaven's name will I ever earn a living
with this face
wondering and sullen.

Elizabeth Nannestad

Chip

Paul whose dad said
watch your language, don't
go getting any
big ideas.

1) A small piece removed.
2) The place where such a chip has been made.

Paul's dad, and Paul.
He let him know all about it
He gave him a piece of his mind.

Andrew Johnston

A Birthday Bow-Wow Blues

As a man grow older
His dog grows sadder

Not as many bow-wows, boy,
Not as many bones. . . .

If you're feeling old
This man he's feeling sad

His happy tales told,
His best times had.

Sam Hunt

Moonshine

The lights in the farmhouses
go out. The inlet is out.

An iron shack on the shoreline
floats its light on the water.

A grandfather up Moonshine
remembers the first daughter.

Dreams are easy. Wild horses.

Sam Hunt

Grandparents

Their language
has the intimacy
of a chronic cough.

Birth and birthplace
are said from the chest.

They are words you know
but can't speak, sounds
your throat won't make.

Angela Andrews

Night

The night is a white song.
You turn in your sleep
and suck it through your mouth.
Inside you it grows like a child.

Albert Wendt

Eleven Days

The rotten flesh-stump that joined us
has fallen off.
I haven't washed her.
I haven't healed.
In these early days, wrapt in our own salty language,
we swear a fealty
I know we cannot rely on.

Anna Livesey

Not less by dreaming more

We dream that we can make summer
Our cloth and paper house does not fall
Even the slow death of the garden is less

Small birds singing: medlar, almond
and pine shaken into planetary explosions
of song we catch against waking

We are not less by dreaming more; on
the back wall a bell with light inside
it where there was none before

Michael Harlow

Time, when you write

for Allen and Jeny

Time, when you write, grows burrs
And on each word this invisible brake
Thickens the moments you work in.

A fast thought burns hours.
A failure to brake at crossroads
Burns the air, the hour until

The air almost smokes or smells of fuel.
The real burr on the animal crossing a field
Is as slow and leisurely as sunlight.

Elizabeth Smither

‘Now is the Month of Maying’

The sky has gone dead.
The park crunches underfoot.
The English trees are going to pieces again.

C.K. Stead

Forest Song

makomako kāmahi tōwai mataī
kōwhai kawakawa ramarama maire
māhoe kaikōmako horopito māpou
mingimingi karaka tarata karo
kiekie mangemange hangehange rātā
pūriri kauri nīkau tōtara
miro kaikawaka kahikatea
rimu tānekaha neinei whau

Janis Freegard

Felled Trees

Nobody has come to burn them,
Long green grass grows up between them,
Up between white boughs that lie
Dead and empty, dry,
That once were full of leaves and sky.

Ruth Dallas

Prime Time

1.

Evening clouds like schools of thought;
great philosophers put to good use
changing the light bulbs up there—
clear, or pearl? They always choose pearl.

2.

'The grey clouds and the pink
elope through dusk to marry in the dark'—
the clematis, for this sentence,
awards itself white stars.

Andrew Johnston

In the far away distance
I can hear the telephone wires
Singing in churches
Like pakehas

Mary (12)

Wingatui

Sit in the car with the headlights off.
Look out there now
where the yellow moon floats silks across the birdcage.
You might have touched that sky you lost.
You might have split that azure violin in two.

Bill Manhire

Jack Without Magic

Clever than ever your busy brain,
Nature you dread, and next to nature, art:
Jack without magic springs his traps in vain
Against these giants and genii of the heart.

Allen Curnow

Metal

Why
For the downward curve
Of the brass spout on a copper coffee-pot
Does delight so upwards swerve?
To ask
But not to take reply
Save from the heart that's learned what falling means,
Save from the sense
Of clouded splendour, rearing, plunging on.

Hubert Witheford

Booty

Ah not as plains that spread into us slowly
But as that mountain flinging at the skies
And not as merchantmen which trundle in the offing
But as a privateer that boards a prize,
Let some come always at me and not to me
And, coming, let it plunder, burn, and flay,
For beauty like heaven by violence is taken
And the violent shall bear it away.

Eileen Duggan

Anorexia

these are the acts of power
to give birth   to kill

you have a new notion

*

in a monochrome of beige sheep & paddocks
you try to say your unclear thing

you curl up like a wild rabbit

*

living out now in the open
you are the original food

Bernadette Hall

Night

You are the still caesura
That breaks a line in two;
A quiet leaf of darkness
Between two flowers of blue;

A little soft indrawing
Between two sighs;
A slender spit of silence
Between two seas of cries.

Eileen Duggan

Sky

If the sky knew half
of what we're doing
down here

it would be stricken,
inconsolable,
and we would have

nothing but rain

Brian Turner

The Mess We Made at Port Chalmers

Tongue-stump of headland bandaged with concrete,
Obliterated beaches stacked with chopsticks.

All of this takes place in shallow time.

In deep time, the trees have already recovered the hills
and the machines rust, immobile, flaking away.
Healing, the land has shifted in its sleep.

All we would see if we were here
is seed-pods moving on the water.

Cilla McQueen

Today

It's a calm day on earth, almost silent.
Only the birds are singing.

Why don't people go down to the harbour,
stand at the end of the earth's long breath
and listen?

Dinah Hawken

The Pool

Ripples from a stone
Dropped in a pool
Like a poem's meaning
Go travelling on

Ruth Dallas

A Visiting Card

How lightly we
carry ourselves

that stirring in
the long grass yes

five minutes ago
that was us.

Gregory O'Brien

Tokens

The sheets have been laundered clean
of our joint essence—a compound,
not a mixture, but here are still

your forgotten pipe and tobacco,
your book open on my table,
your voice speaking in my poems.

Fleur Adcock

Tidal

for Meg, 1937–2007

I made this poem for you
Out of tidal wrack.
I spoke my lines to the wind,
And the wind blew them back.

This is my last poem.
It's out there on the beach
For the first high tide to turn
And float it out of reach.

Alistair Te Ariki Campbell

What shall I do with it, with
this that comes and is so strange
and different, so difficult to put
in its place?

Helen Shaw

A Song of Innocence

Morning Song for Hecate

Should I serve up a breakfast for somebody's daughter,
just the right size like . . . say, a mouse and a quarter?

Kendrick Smithyman

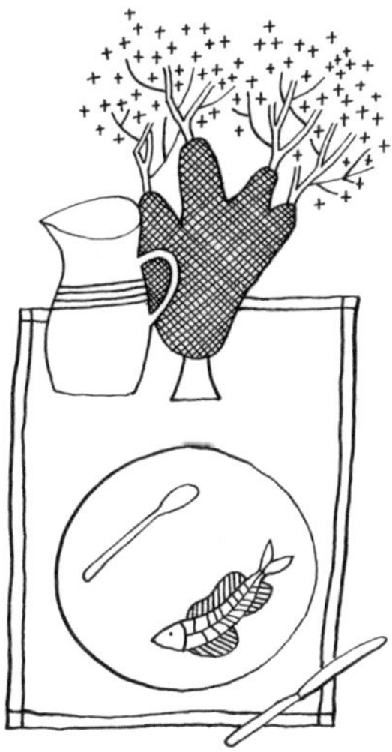

Haiku (2)

To a tree cling
lonely
bird and leaf

Go bird and leaf:
shake
the sad tree

Hone Tuwhare

The Elaboration

There was a way out of here:
it went off in the night
licking its lips.

The door flaps like a great wing:
I make fists at the air
and long to weaken.

Ah, to visit you
is the plain thing,
and I shall not come to it.

Bill Manhire

Rooms

We embrace forever in each of the rooms.
An open window pulls sheets from the bed.
The pictureless walls are singing their freedoms.
I try to see your face but your face is pressed into my shoulder.
Silence leads us into the rest of our lives
which are deep pools where we cannot touch our feet
and cannot move our arms so much,
where we are naked and cannot take so much from each other.

Ashleigh Young

All the Keys in the World

Common law says
ownership extends
to the centre of the earth
and to the stars.

All things have their ends.
A battery dies
and all the keys in the world
won't turn that engine over.

Kate Camp

from Six Roman Poems

Yes, I am a bitter old stick.
I can hear it too. Starchy.

                    Oh, but
Kissed in the right places
how lacking in all that I can be.

Elizabeth Nannestad

from Seferis

In a small garden—they don’t
come much smaller—light strikes
two red carnations, as it strikes
a sliver of honeysuckle, a single olive.

Light is where you are.

Vincent O’Sullivan

You gave me a shoulder

smelling of the sun
I can bite on, or weep.

What can I give you
so it's fair?

Take
my rough, unsteady
compassion while you sleep.

Elizabeth Nannestad

meditation on blue

sudden spears of
Agapanthus open
blue on grey
Pohutukawa
with the violence of
love in a
quiet life

Joanna Margaret Paul

Lines Written in Absence

Against the Lodestone of your mouth
Chaos received a North and South:

But now a favourite Book you lie
Open before my Loving eye,
And on each Leaf, each page I turn
Incendiary memories burn.

Denis Glover

The Forecast for Night

Showers, though their rhythms may be
Interrupted by wind and gusts
Will not cease in the dark hours
They should continue until first light.

Going to sleep one imagines a dance
With interruptions, a shouldering
A standing to one side, a sweeping
Together and deeper into different arms.

Elizabeth Smither

Scrap

As I pass Evans Bay the shore shows me
its debris of seaweed shells driftwood
fragments of rusted anchors and boat ribs
plastic bags cigarette packets
indefinable salt detritus piled high
on the stones. Gulls on the grass
by the road peck like hens
in the dirty backyard of the storm.

Lauris Edmond

Nexus

The moon, full and September,
Runs the night's cool stain.
Like a radiologist's image
I would rather not remember,
my love, walking on the white road,
darkens pure bone.

Vincent O'Sullivan

Mātai rore au

Mātai rore au ki te taumata,
Te ngakau whakapuke tonu.
Me aha iho ka mauru ai,
Whiuwhiu kei te muri, kei te tonga?

On the hill tops

On the hill tops I visit the snares,
And my heart keeps surging up.
Oh how can I quiet my heart,
That is tossed from north to south?

Traditional, translated by Margaret Orbell

Before I Get into Sleep with You

Before I get into sleep with you
I want to have been
into wakefulness, too.

Janet Frame

View from the House of Many Chimneys

Tables and streams and chairs
a setting. Imagine a painted rock

thrown into a painted river.
What shall I do with this

sleep? Where can I leave it
so she will find it?

Gregory O'Brien

The Hour

is empty.
Should I fill it
with the wing beats
of small birds?

Stephanie de Montalk

Radio

Now we are alone at last,
You and I together,
Talk to me, 3YA,
Tell me about the weather.

Denis Glover

Seven wishes

A straight account is difficult
so let me define seven wishes:

that you should fit inside me neat as the stuffing in an olive
that you should stand inside the safe circle of my eye
that you should sing, clear, on the high rock of my skull
that you should swing wide on the rope of my hair
that you should cross rivers of blood, mountains of bone
that I should touch your skin through the hole in your tee shirt
that we should exchange ordinary tales.

Fiona Farrell

The Order of Things

Red tulips drooping in the park.
Remarkable how quickly things change:
It's tomorrow.
                              It's today.

Lynley Edmeades

yellowing out
one week
greening in
the next
Babylonian (won’t
you) hang up
your heart
willow willow
and stay

Michele Leggott

Someone mentions your name

I hear a faraway tune strange accordion music that
needs to be cranked and just as quickly it's gone again
like sand in the wind shooting up off dunes the same way
that you left me I gasp I suck in air like soba greedy
giddy on my great escape how good how good this tastes

Louise Wallace

From One Centre

Where I went for watercress stank of cattle
but I wanted it (metaphor)

An insect leg drops on the page.
Thought it was a little twig but it had joints.

A week ago I threw Kên and Tui:
strong lines of change.

Oh these affairs of the heart!
If only we could turn to bite the place.

Ian Wedde

Our love was a grim citadel

Our love was a grim citadel:
    no tawdry plaything for the minute
    of strong dark stone we built it well
    and based in the ever-living granite:

The urgent columns of the years
    press on like tall rain up the valley:
    and Chaos bids ten thousand spears
    run to erase our straw-built folly.

R.A.K. Mason

Things

There are worse things than having behaved foolishly in public.
There are worse things than these miniature betrayals,
committed or endured or suspected; there are worse things
than not being able to sleep for thinking about them.
It is 5 a.m. All the worse things come stalking in
and stand icily about the bed looking worse and worse and worse.

Fleur Adcock

Beak

The curlew haunts the seashores and moorlands, carrying its marks of distinction, the beak and the plaintive cry.

Imagine me as that little bird,
legs holding me up, wings
a folded possibility, beak
investigating under stones and sometimes
opening to let out
the sound of a sad heart.

Anna Livesey

Remembering Summer

The memory of what you'd love to do again
    is on the rise. You'd run barefoot
over the grass on a summer's evening,

the sky like candy in the west
    where the wind and the sun die down,
watch light flickering in the bounce

of water flowing over a cobbly bed
    of gorgeous yellow, green and brown stones,
your mother's voice calling you home.

Brian Turner

How Memory Works

Come over here
we say to the days that disappear.

No, over here.

Bill Manhire

My Mother Spinning

Sit too close
& the spinning bobbin cools you.
Leave the room
& the foot pedal beats
on a raw nerve.
Leave the house

& a thread of wool follows.

Peter Olds

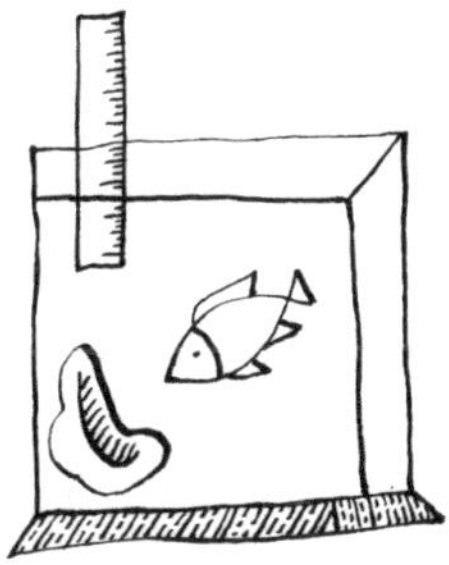

Adultery in the Age of Pisces

How does it go, Lord?
How does the old song go?
Didn't we love you enough, Lord,
when you were a little fish?

Cliff Fell

Closer

My Dear,
Goodbye.

They are wild for repetition.

There is nothing
save you
and the fictitious stars.

James Brown

Cairn

Rusty knuckled iron remains,
the paddock cleared of stones.
Haft, shaft, bucket,
imperium, lode. His hand
on the language, hers on the hoe.

Bernadette Hall

Early Settler Song

Where is the girl
with the grateful curls?
—the treasure buried in paradise?
Where is the map?
and the cook? and the ship?
and where are the pirates they promised?

James Brown

Stone

o
on earth there is more than
one chance to sing out, to find the right
tone, to be struck down by who you are—a single
stone on a beach of stones. Do nothing. A calm, clamouring
tone comes with sea-surge. Be smoothed. Be
one of the ones rattling and tumbling around
on the swell, in the sorrow, in the interim
o

Dinah Hawken

Without Form

for Marion

It is noisiest here in this middle place,
cries of despair and those of praise,
yet you might close your eyes and begin to walk forward.

This must be how the first god did it.
It was back at the beginning, and he began to sing,
Though the light—which was there—showed nothing.

Bill Manhire

An Ambulance

Between hospital and zoo
asterisks of rain fall audibly
on the many old tin awnings.
Through cool blue air arrives
a siren's pure ambulance. Someone
is dying of too much afternoon,
of fennel and cats and clothes props.

Geoff Cochrane

Hole

Wind blows in space,
we ask questions
about how and why?
The plastic cover flaps
an answer from the wind;
rain melts tape
and dark streets slip in.

Mary Macpherson

Concrete City

The concrete city is demolished; clothes and utensils lie in the street. A young couple are trying to find their house. There is the smell of burnt meat as ash settles in their hair.

It's only a burning tiger. The zoo keeper sits on a tin of petrol and weeps. He must hang the giraffes before the Americans come.

James McNaughton

Brooding

Ah lift yourself from your own pain
And think of others' misery.
It is a swamp that sours in rain.
The good land drains into the sea.

Eileen Duggan

Ah, sweet life, We share it
with cancers and tapeworms
with bread moulds and string beans
and great white sharks . . .

Keri Hulme

Out in the Garden

Out in the garden,
Out in the windy, swinging dark,
Under the trees and over the flower-beds,
Over the grass and under the hedge border,
Someone is sweeping, sweeping,
Some old gardener.
Out in the windy, swinging dark,
Someone is secretly putting in order,
Someone is creeping, creeping.

Katherine Mansfield

The Acolyte

My quiet morning hill
    Stands like an altar drawn
Whereon hushed hands shall lay
    The shining pyx of dawn.

With penitence and stir,
    And drowsy flurry by,
The wind, a shamefaced serving-boy,
    Comes running up the sky.

Eileen Duggan

Prepare

Not yet came spring, but the last lap of winter.
Storms. Hail. Rain. Rain. Rain.
Flowers all swept down. Birds silent.

Then much hard toil. Much backache.
Muddy boots. Scratched hands. Deep sleep.

Then one morning a general greenness,
And all the rose-bushes broken into leaf—

Ursula Bethell

from haiku & senryu

early spring—
buttoning   unbuttoning
my jacket

John O'Connor

text message

up close and matesy with warbler
this morning letting me watch
no worries not shy warbling
followed by thundering farm trucks
probably filled with little lambs
it's
the slaughtering season

Sam Duckor-Jones

Sea Change

Spring and the come-back glow
shifts, blue-green and red-tinged blue,
light hits the undersea bed.
I could lose my footing
on this clay bank, taking my mind
from my step, going over and over
the last time we met. The sun
                roaring in my head.

Rhian Gallagher

Tangi te kawekaweā

Tangi te kawekaweā—waiho kia tangi ana!
  Tangi te wharauroa—waiho kia tangi ana!
  E tatari atu ana kia aroara-mahana, ka taka mai te āhuru!
  Kōia!

Planting spell

The long-tailed cuckoo sings—let it sing!
  The shining cuckoo sings—let it sing!
  They are waiting for the summer, when the warmth will come!
  Dig!

Traditional, translated by Margaret Orbell

Listening

with a microphone plugged into the earth
we can hear ferns creaking, rabbit-chatter,
tree roots muscling up through the dirt.

We can hear bones turning, slugs spawning,
mushrooms growing, ants drinking sap.
When we take our earphones off we can hear

earth's huge silence listening back.

Peter Bland

Detail

My garage is a structure of excessive plainness,
It springs from a dry bank in the back garden,
It is made of corrugated iron,
And painted all over with brick-red.

But beside it I have planted a green Bay-tree,
—A sweet Bay, an Olive, and a Turkey Fig,
—A fig, an Olive, and a Bay.

Ursula Bethell

Poppies

Tight-folded in each oval pack,
   Pale green, and haired with bristles black,
These poppy flowers wait
   Till the hot signal of the sun
Unbuckles them; then, one by one
   Their crumpled parachutes released
With silken shapes all seamed and creased
   And many-coloured flare,
Tethered to earth, will float upon the air.

Basil Dowling

The School for Sopranos

An old building,
the staircase winding up through the centre,
like the voices of the novices, circling
for a note.

Anna Livesey

Notes

How flaky to decide
to compose you as music
when I can’t even sing.
Or play an instrument.
That’s why we have pop.
Here come your notable legs
—right on song.
All the leaves are *green*

James Brown

Aesthetic

Yellow daisy, yellow daisy, where have I known you?
Something comes back to me from a far distant past—
Now I remember you were painted on a mantel-piece,
A Victorian mantel-piece, on a green background,
By one called Ethel, out of Thackeray.

Ursula Bethell

Stubble Fields

for Ian Reid

In some stubble fields an indentation
Perhaps a small swamp dried in summer
Traces a faint black imperfect sowing
Like a panda's eye.

Fields that contain these small infelicities
Are more beautiful than the perfect
Skinhead fields they emulate
More individual, with a love-bite.

Elizabeth Smither

The back gate of Solway College, thirty years on

The view of the chapel is not even
altered from where I'm standing.

The attack-magpie waits in the tree
twisting its neck to see everything as it was

through a strange shaft of light opening
onto our stucco sunbathing wall.

Where are Joy and Darlene, coconut-oiled
or Dawn with her secret scar?

Marty Smith

Kelburn Park

The grass shaggy already,
white lines partitioning the field
to other codes, enigmas.

The square is invisible.
A huddle of grey-backed gulls,
a hunch of slips and short legs.

The nets look deserted, but if you squint
there's Hamish just taking guard,
Tony sidling up to bowl.

Harry Ricketts

shifting points

look see
here it is

what's
to happen

now that's
forgotten

Lindsay Rabbitt

drawing a conclusion on a paper dart

such is the language
of exigency

you wash & cut
& core yellow pears

you could do
with a pig

white & cool
as ointment

the lawn is
littered with them

Bernadette Hall

Opening

There is too much
poetry in the world

and yet

here you are.

James Brown

Acknowledgements

Fleur Adcock: 'Tokens', 'Things' from *Poems 1960–2000* (Bloodaxe Books, 2000).

Michele Amas: 'Temporary Beds' from *After the Dance* (Victoria University Press, 2006).

Angela Andrews: 'Grandparents' from *Echolocation* (Victoria University Press, 2007).

Tusiata Avia: 'Waiting for my brother' from *Wild Dogs Under My Skirt* (Victoria University Press, 2004).

Hinemoana Baker: 'Referee' from *mātuhi|needle* (Victoria University Press, 2004).

James K. Baxter: 'High Country Weather' from *Collected Poems* (Oxford University Press, 1979).

Ursula Bethell: 'Detail', 'Prepare', 'Aesthetic' from *Collected Poems* (Victoria University Press, 1997).

Tony Beyer: 'Lord Cobham Avenue' from *Brute Music* (Hard Echo Press, 1984).

Peter Bland: 'Listening' from 'Poems for Jo' from *Collected Poems 1956–2011* (Steele Roberts, 2012).

Charles Brasch: 'Rain over Mitimiti Mountains' from *Selected Poems* chosen by Alan Roddick (Otago University Press, 2015).

Diana Bridge: 'Carved Couple' from *Red Leaves* (Auckland University Press, 2005).

Sarah Broom: 'Panther' from *Tigers at Awhitu* (Auckland University Press, 2010).

James Brown: 'Opening' from *Floods Another Chamber* (Victoria University Press, 2017); 'Early Settler Song' from *Go Round Power Please* (Victoria University Press, 1995); 'Notes', 'Closer' from *Lemon* (Victoria University Press, 1999).

Rachel Bush: '22 March '96', extract from short poem series 'Truth Tables' in *The Hungry Woman* (Victoria University Press, 1997), 'Still' from *Thought Horses* (Victoria University Press, 2016).

Kate Camp: 'All the Keys in the World' from *Realia* (Victoria University Press, 2001); 'Bumper stickers' from *Unfamiliar Legends of the Stars* (Victoria University Press, 1998).

Alistair Te Ariki Campbell: 'Dreams, Yellow Lions', 'Tidal', 'Friend:' from *The Collected Poems of Alistair Te Ariki Campbell* (Victoria University Press, 2016).

Geoff Cochrane: 'Motel' from *84-484* (Victoria University Press, 2007); 'Suicide Abroad', 'An Ambulance' from *Aztec Noon Poems 1976–1992* (Victoria University Press, 1992); '*Savvy meters clack their blank eyes shut*' from *Vanilla Wine* (Victoria University Press, 2003).

Allen Curnow: 'Wild Iron', 'Jack Without Magic' from *Collected Poems* (Auckland University Press, 2017).

Ruth Dallas: 'Felled Trees', 'The Pool' from *Collected Poems* (University of Otago Press, 2000).

Stephanie de Montalk: 'The Hour' from *Cover Stories* (Victoria University Press, 2005).

Basil Dowling: 'Poppies' from *A Book of New Zealand Verse 1923–50,* ed. Allen Curnow (The Caxton Press, 1951). With permission from Imogen Jasch and Virginia Strauss.

Sam Duckor-Jones: 'text message' from *People from the Pit Stand Up* (Victoria University Press, 2018).

Eileen Duggan: 'The Acolyte', 'Brooding', 'Night', 'Booty' from *Eileen Duggan Selected Poems,* ed. Peter Whiteford (Victoria University Press, 1994).

Lynley Edmeades: 'East Belfast', 'The Order of Things' from *As the Verb Tenses* (Otago University Press, 2016).

Lauris Edmond: 'Scrap' from *Scenes from a Small City* (Daphne Brasell Associates Press, 1994).

Murray Edmond: 'Cookbook' from *From The Word Go* (Auckland University Press, 1992).

David Eggleton: 'Big City Rush Hour' from *South Pacific Sunrise* (Penguin Books, 1986); 'Roadkill' from *The Conch Trumpet* (Otago University Press, 2015).

A.R.D. Fairburn: 'In the Younger Land' from *A Book of New Zealand Verse 1923–45* chosen by Allen Curnow (The Caxton Press, 1945).

Fiona Farrell [Poole]: 'Seven wishes' from *Cutting Out* (Auckland University Press, 1987).

Cliff Fell: 'Adultery in the Age of Pisces' from *The Adulterer's Bible* (Victoria University Press, 2003).

Janet Frame: 'The Chickadee', 'Before I Get into Sleep with You', from *The Goose Bath* (Vintage, 2006, reprinted in *Storms Will Tell*, Bloodaxe Books, 2008). With copyright permission from the Janet Frame Literary Trust.

Janis Freegard: 'Forest Song', from *The Glass Rooster* (Auckland University Press, 2015).

Rhian Gallagher: 'Sea Change' from *Shift* (Auckland University Press, 2011).

Denis Glover: 'Wellington at 5 O'Clock', 'Radio' from *Sharp Edge Up: Verses & Satires* (Blackwood & Janet Paul, 1968); 'Lines Written in Absence' from *Enter Without Knocking* (The Pegasus Press, 1964); 'Home Thoughts', from *Denis Glover Selected Poems,* ed. Bill Manhire (Victoria University Press, 1995).

Paula Green: 'cherry pie' from *Cookhouse* (Auckland University Press, 1997).

Rob Hack: 'Bring your camera ay?' from *Everything Is Here* (Escalator Press, 2016).

Bernadette Hall: 'Anorexia', 'Cairn', 'drawing a conclusion on a paper dart' from *the merino princess: selected poems* (Victoria University Press, 2004); 'Under Erebus' from *The Ponies* (Victoria University Press, 2007); 'Cromwell' from *The Lustre Jug* (Victoria University Press, 2009).

Michael Harlow: 'Not less by dreaming more' from *Sweeping the Courtyard* (Cold Hub Press, 2014).

Dinah Hawken: '*from* The Harbour Poems', 'Today' from *Oh There You Are, Tui!: New and Selected Poems* (Victoria University Press, 2001); 'Stone' from *Ocean and Stone* (Victoria University Press, 2015).

Keri Hulme: '*I asked for riches*' from *The Silences Between (Moeraki Conversations)* (Auckland University Press/Oxford University Press, 1982); '*Ah, sweet life, We share it*' from *Strands* (Auckland University Press, 1992).

Sam Hunt: 'A Birthday Bow-Wow Blues', 'Moonshine', from *Collected Poems* (Penguin Books Ltd, 1981).

Andrew Johnston: 'Prime Time' from *The Sounds* (Victoria University Press, 1996); 'Chip' from *The Open Window* (Arc Publications International Poets, 1999).

Michele Leggott: '*yellowing out*' from *Like This* (Caxton Press, 1988).

Anna Livesey: 'The School for Sopranos', 'Beak', 'Foreshore, Evening' from *Good Luck* (Victoria University Press, 2003); 'What Licence Issued You Away?' from *The Moonmen* (Victoria University Press, 2010); 'Eleven Days' from *Ordinary Time* (Victoria University Press, 2017).

Therese Lloyd: 'Everest' from *Other Animals* (Victoria University Press, 2013).

Bill Manhire: 'The Elaboration', 'Poem', 'Wingatui', 'Without Form' from *Selected Poems* (Victoria University Press, 2012); 'How Memory Works', 'My World War I Poem' from *Some Things to Place in a Coffin* (Victoria University Press, 2017).

Katherine Mansfield: 'Out in the Garden' from *Poems of Katherine Mansfield*, ed. O'Sullivan (Oxford University Press, 1988).

Mary Macpherson: 'Beach', 'Holes' from *the inland eye* (Pemmican Press, 1998).

Mary (12): '*In the far away distance*' originally published in *From the Early World*, ed. Elwyn Richardson (1964), from *100 New Zealand Poems*, ed. Bill Manhire (Godwit Press, 1993).

R.A.K. Mason: 'Our love was a grim citadel' from *Collected Poems: R.A.K Mason* (Victoria University Press, 1990).

Maria McMillan: 'The avalanche' from *The Ski Flier* (Victoria University Press, 2017).

James McNaughton: 'Concrete City' from *The Stepmother Tree* (Darius Press, 2001).

Cilla McQueen: 'The Mess We Made at Port Chalmers' from *Axis: Poems and Drawings* (University of Otago Press, 2001).

Elizabeth Nannestad: '"You're Just a Dreamer"', 'You gave me a shoulder' from *Jump* (Auckland University Press, 1986); '*from* Six Roman Poems' from *If He's a Good Dog He'll Swim* (Auckland University Press, 1996).

Gregory O'Brien: 'View From the House of Many Chimneys' from *Great Lake* (Local Consumption Publications, 1991); 'On Rapanui (Easter Island)' from *Whale Years* (Auckland University Press, 2015); 'A Visiting Card' from *Location of the Least Person* (Auckland University Press, 1987).

John O'Connor: '*from* haiku and senryu' from *A Particular Context* (Sudden Valley Press, 1999).

Peter Olds: 'My Mother Spinning' from *It Was a Tuesday Morning—Selected Poems 1972–2001* (Hazard Press, 2004).

Margaret Orbell (translator): 'Mātai rore au' / 'On the hill tops', 'Tangi te kawekaweā' / 'Planting spell' from *Maori Poetry—an introductory anthology*, ed. Margaret Orbell (Heinemann Educational Books (NZ) Ltd, 1978).

Bob Orr: 'Ariel' from *Poems for Moira* (Hawk Press, 1979).

Chris Orsman: 'Cape Gooseberries' from *White Wind* (Pemmican Press, 2001).

Vincent O'Sullivan: 'from Seferis' from *The movie may be slightly different* (Victoria University Press, 2011); 'Nexus', 'Remembering Mrs Hardy', 'Watching the Hawkduns' from *Further Convictions Pending: Poems 1998–2008* (Victoria University Press, 2009).

Joanna Margaret Paul: 'Meditation on Blue' from *Like Love Poems* (Victoria University Press, 2006).

John Pule: '*I was born with*', '*When I came to your shore*' from *Sadness Spirit* (Pataka Art Museum, 2013).

Lindsay Rabbitt: 'shifting points' from *thewayofit* (Black Robin Press, 1988).

Harry Ricketts: 'Kelburn Park' from *Just Then* (Victoria University Press, 2012).

Frances Samuel: 'Balagan', 'Anorexia' from *Sleeping on Horseback* (Victoria University Press, 2014).

Helen Shaw: '*What shall I do with it*' from *I Listen: Reflections & meditations,* ed. Deborah Grossman Knowles (Puriri Press, 1995).

Marty Smith: 'The back gate of Solway College, thirty years on' from *Horse With Hat* (Victoria University Press, 2014).

Elizabeth Smither: 'Stubble Fields', 'A Small Seascape in Oils', 'The Forecast for Night' from *A Pattern of Marching* (Auckland University Press, 1989); 'Time, when you write' from *The Tudor Style: Poems new and selected* (Auckland University Press, 1993).

Kendrick Smithyman: 'A Song of Innocence' from *Auto/Biographies* (Auckland University Press, 1992).

C.K. Stead: '"Now is the Month of Maying"', 'On Turning Seventy' from *Collected Poems, 1951–2006* (Auckland University Press, 2008; Carcanet, 2009).

Robert Sullivan: 'Sitting in front of the Karetu Marae' from *Piki Ake! Poems 1990–92* (Auckland University Press, 1993).

Brian Turner: 'Remembering Summer' from *Taking Off* (Victoria University Press, 2001); 'Sky' from *Just This* (Victoria University Press, 2009).

Hone Tuwhare: 'Haiku (1)', 'Haiku (2)', 'Sapwood and Milk' from *Small Holes in the Silence: Collected Works* (Penguin Random House New Zealand, 2011).

Arnold Wall: 'The City from the Hills' from *The Penguin Book of New Zealand Verse*, ed. Allen Curnow (Penguin, 1960).

Louise Wallace: 'Introductions' from *Since June* (Victoria University Press, 2009); 'Someone mentions your name' from *Sport* 44 (Victoria University Press, 2015).

Ian Wedde: 'From One Centre' from *Tales of Gotham City* (Auckland University Press/Oxford University Press, 1984); 'Tony's Tyre Service' from *Selected Poems* (Auckland University Press, 2017).

Albert Wendt: 'Night' from 'Short Songs' from *Shaman of Visions* (Auckland University Press/Oxford University Press, 1984).

Hubert Witheford: 'Metal' from *The Lightning Makes a Difference* (The Brookside Press, London, 1962).

Ashleigh Young: 'Rooms' from *Cyphers* 81, eds Leland Bardwell, Pearse Hutchinson, Eiléan Ní Chuilleanáin and Macdara Woods (May 2016).

Index